The Youth Libraries Committee of The Library Association

Children and Young People

Library Association Guidelines for Public Library Services

Second Edition

Working Group
Gill Johnson, *Chair*, Catherine Blanshard, *editor*, Carl Earl, Anne Everall, Margaret Fraser, Sue Greenfield, Carol Holmes, Mary Knowles, David Lathrope, Alec Williams

Library Association Publishing
London

© The Library Association 1991, 1997

Library Association Publishing is wholly owned by The Library Association

Published by
Library Association Publishing
7 Ridgmount Street
London WC1E 7AE

First published 1991
Second edition 1997

British Library Cataloguing in Publication Data
A catalogue record for this book is available from the British Library

ISBN 1-85604-209-X

Typeset in Garamond and Avant Garde by Library Association Publishing. Printed and made in Great Britain by Rexam Digital Imaging Ltd, Reading, Berkshire.

Contents

Foreword

Library services for children and young people have never been so important. Our society is varied and complex, and knowledge of the wider world is increasingly important. We are all engaged in lifelong learning and, in some fields, children already know more than parents and teachers. Five hundred years ago, most people could learn about the world from their own families, and parents could pass on to their children the skills they needed to survive. Even 50 years ago, many parents attempted to do the same. Now, we cannot predict what our children will need to know. If their development is not to be stunted, we must give them independent access to the knowledge and cultural riches of the world.

That, of course, is what public libraries provide, and there can be no doubt that children welcome that provision, in all its forms. Scaremongers try to suggest that young people are bored with books, but the facts tell a different tale. In a period of reduced borrowing by adults, the number of public library books issued to children continues to rise. Children are quick to master new media (and we should all be glad of that) but they also appreciate traditional sources of information and entertainment.

Their enthusiasm does not mean, however, that public libraries are perfect. Like all information services, libraries must respond constantly to changes in the needs of their users and in the world around. In addition, in this country, public libraries have had to weather alterations in the organization and financing of local government; and children's services have also been deeply affected by recent developments in education. Being concerned about the problems caused by these changes, and recognizing the importance of library services to children and young people, the Library and Information Services Council (England) set up a working party which produced the report *Investing in children* in 1995.

These new Guidelines are one of the major responses to that report. They deal thoroughly and thoughtfully with the issues raised by *Investing in children* and establish a sound and detailed basis for the future. Their careful teasing out of complicated issues (such as the relationship of public libraries, school libraries and schools library services) is matched by a firm grasp of basic essentials, like the importance of appropriate staffing and good stock selection policies. Their emphasis on strategic planning and the need to adapt to new situations is both helpful and challenging.

Above all, however, the Guidelines focus on children and young people themselves, never losing sight of the joyful exploration of reality which is at the heart of childhood. Assisting that exploration is one of the pleasures and duties of adult life and these Guidelines provide a thoughtful view of how to achieve that better. We should all celebrate their publication.

Gillian Cross

Gillian Cross is a member of the Advisory Council on Libraries, and served
on the LISC Working Party which produced the report *Investing in children*.

Recommendations

The Library Association recommends that:

1 The child and the library

Consideration of children, and what libraries can add to their quality of life, must inform and determine the nature of public library services to children and young people (2.1).

The special features and circumstances of childhood justify library consideration of children as a specific (though not necessarily separated) client group (2.2.1).

The library's responsibility must be to the local child population as a whole and not its current users alone (2.4.1).

Children from all backgrounds, cultures and abilities have an equal right of access to library services (2.4.1).

Work with children must be seen as an integral part of the whole range of library services (2.4.2).

Services to children should be seen as part of a continuum of service to individuals throughout their lives (2.4.2).

All aspects of the library service must agree a consistent and positive policy for child users (2.4.2).

Children's services must be seen as being part of the responsibility of all staff (2.4.2).

Given the nature of the client group, posts with specialist knowledge, training and experience have an important part to play in the delivery of library services (2.4.2).

The children's service requires clear sense of purpose, aims and objectives and strategic plans for client groups and service provision (2.4.3).

2 Service entitlement

A statement for children identifying what the library will offer them should be considered (3.2).

Service strategy for under-fives, children and young people, and children with special needs should be created, identifying aims and objectives (3.3–3.6).

The library should provide and promote material which assists reading development in young children (3.8.1).

Events should be organized which enhance literacy (3.8.2).

Libraries should provide and promote services which assist those with literacy difficulties (3.8.3).

Consulting with children is vital for future development of services. It helps give them democratic opportunity and it ensures services are appropriate and relevant (3.9).

3 Specifying the service

Clear measurable standards need to be set for all aspects of library provision. Local libraries should then set targets to reach these standards (4.2).

A monitoring and evaluation system is required to ensure relevance of standards and to measure development of libraries (4.4).

4 Relationship between service providers

There should be a clear understanding of the different services provided by the school library, the public library service and the schools library service (5.2).

An integrated strategy of services to children should accompany this (5.3).

5 Planning and design

To ensure the effective planning and design of children's libraries, it is important that a senior member of staff with considerable experience of library work with children is involved in the planning process from the earliest stage (6.1).

In planning and designing a children's library, careful consideration needs to be given to questions of siting (6.2), size of area required (6.4), safety (6.7), consultation (6.9) and choice of furniture (6.6).

To ensure continuity for children using adult library areas, planning and design decisions should be coordinated (6.8).

6 Staffing

The staffing resources should have the knowledge, skills and expertise that are essential to the development, promotion and delivery of a high quality service to children (7.2).

A responsibility for an awareness of how to relate to and deal with children should be required of all public library service staff (7.3).

Training in work with children should be part of both introductory and cyclical training programmes for all staff (7.5).

In terms of access to library provision and services, children should have equality of opportunity with all other client groups (7.3).

The staffing structure must reflect a policy which supports and defines each authority's public library provision to children (7.4).

There needs to be a clear line management structure in terms of delivery of the service and the means by which policy is formulated, implemented and evaluated (7.4).

It is strongly recommended that each authority should have a specialist post at a senior management level with overall responsibility for coordinating, managing, developing and monitoring services to children (7.4).

The employment of specialists other than at senior management level, including to those in regular contact with children, is also recommended (7.4).

7 Stock

In determining stock provision it is important to build up a clear picture of the community comprising each library's catchment area (8.2).

It is strongly recommended that all library authorities should draw up a written stock policy document. This should state very clearly the objectives underlying stock provision (8.3) and should give guidance relating to the range (8.5), format (8.6), size (8.8) and composition of stock (8.9) at each service point, together with stock circulation (8.12).

A stock selection policy should be formulated which is agreed between library management and those staff responsible for selection (8.4).

The development of an effective maintenance plan is of vital importance (8.11).

The effectiveness of the stock policy should be evaluated as part of an on-going process (8.13).

An IT policy is vital (8.7).

8 Promotion

Promotional strategies should be built into service development at the planning stage (9.1).

All library promotion should meet clear objectives, be carefully targeted, be professional in appearance/delivery and be monitored for impact and effectiveness (9.2).

The promotion of children's library services should reflect the variety of target audiences involved with this client group. These comprise children, parents and carers, teachers, library staff and the profession at large (9.3).

1 Introduction

1.1 Managing change

It would be a mistake to assume that there is an infallible process whereby guidelines for service delivery and development can be made 'future-proof'. In the relatively short period of time since the publication of the first edition in 1991, there have been many outcomes of political, economic, social and technological change which have made an impact on the public library's capability to respond to the library and information needs of children and young people. The pressure has grown to address the resolution of short-term problems as uncertainties about the medium and longer term increase. Whilst it is inevitable that these guidelines will be used to evaluate the present position in service provision, the effective management of change necessitates a longer-term vision of how public library provision for children and young people might develop in the future.

In many ways the *Guidelines* present a paradox; a framework for managing the present whilst at the same time aspiring to provide a platform for progress.

The future will require flexible, adaptable librarians and managers who can manage change proactively and innovatively. It will require tools to manage the paradoxes of the present; children's library services are well supported by the public in principle, but have fewer resources to meet changing needs and increasing demands for books and information. It will require a clear vision and strong direction to lead a service through change. In the process, new ways of thinking about our problems and the future of our services will emerge which will challenge existing conventions. The *Guidelines* provide a common focus for future departures to meet the challenges ahead.

The *Guidelines* are not intended to be prescriptive. Rather they seek to highlight key issues which should form the basis for clear and objective policy statements at a local level. The issues raised are common to all library services irrespective of size, community, structure or political complexion. Aspects covered include philosophy and specification, planning, staff, stock, promotion and equality of access.

Every child has a right of access to a service through the local public library. Article 17 of the United Nations *Convention on the rights of the child*[1] asks member states to '. . . ensure that the child has access to information and material from a diversity of national and international sources' and to this end '. . . to encourage the dissemination of children's books'. Legislation such as the *Public Libraries and Museums Act, 1964*[2] reflects this ('. . . it is the duty of every library authority to provide a comprehensive and efficient library service for all persons . . . [and to] encourage both adults and children to make use of it . . .'), as does the *Public Libraries (Scotland) Act of 1955*.[3]

This document updates the first edition, published in 1991, in response to a recommendation to do so in the report *Investing in children*.[4] It has been compiled by a working group of librarians from a range of local authorities and professional organizations and its recommendations were ratified by The Library Association in 1996.

The *Guidelines* are primarily for use by all those involved in delivering public library services to children. For specialist posts, it is hoped that they stimulate discussion, confirm direction, and provide a basis for training; for Heads of Service, they can provide a touchstone for developing local policy and service strategies. For more general posts, and other specialists, the *Guidelines* can provide an insight into work with children, and how it should integrate within the whole service. Finally, for Chief Officers, it is hoped they provide a useful update on this vital area, and an opportunity for discussion by local Council members.

Finally, there are some points of definition. For the purposes of this document, the age range covered extends from birth to 16. For ease of reference, the client group is referred to simply as *children* throughout, except in those cases where comments apply to under-fives or young people alone. After wide discussion it was decided not to use the word teenager, and the term *young people* is used throughout.

The term *all staff* is used to cover professionally qualified librarians, library managers, senior library assistants, library assistants, drivers, caretakers, Saturday staff, casual relief, volunteers and switchboard staff.

The term *special needs* has been used throughout following much debate. The term covers gifted children, children with disabilities, children with learning difficulties, children with specific language or cultural needs, those geographically isolated and those with a financial or educational disadvantage (see 3.6). There is no generic term to cover all groups of children (it is their individual needs which are important), but for ease of reading we have used this broad term in this document.

These *Guidelines* should be read in conjunction with the following publications: CoSLA, *Standards for public library service in Scotland* (1995),[5] and the LISC (Wales), *Report of a working party on public library services* (1988).[6]

References

1   United Nations, *Convention on the rights of the child*, adopted by the United Nations, 20 November 1989 (Resolution 44/25), and entered into force 2 September 1990.

2   Great Britain, Statutes, *Public Libraries and Museums Act*, Ch. 75, HMSO, 1964.

3   Great Britain, Statutes, *Public Libraries (Scotland) Act*, Ch. 27, HMSO, 1955.

4   Library and Information Services Council (England), *Investing in children*, (DNH Library Information Series No. 22), HMSO, 1995.

5   Convention of Scottish Local Authorities (CoSLA), *Standards for the public library service in Scotland: report of a working group appointed by the Arts and Recreation Committee of CoSLA*, CoSLA, 1995.

6   Library and Information Services Council (Wales), *Report of a working party on public library services*, LISC, 1988.

2 The child and the library

2.1 Introduction

The child has been taken as both a focus and a starting point in these *Guidelines*. It is consideration of children, and what libraries can add to their quality of life, which must inform and determine the nature of library services to children and young people.

2.2 The child

2.2.1 Characteristics of children as a client group

Approximately 10 million, or 20% of the UK population, are aged 16 or under. Statistically, this group is a significant proportion of the total population. Children display a wide variety of different needs and abilities because of the age range involved, and therefore should not be dealt with as a homogeneous group. Children of the same age may display a wide range of interests and abilities. Other factors also need to be considered such as language and culture. Younger children are particularly dependent on parents or other carers. Consequently, library services also need to work through and with these adults. The organizations existing for children's care, education and leisure, such as schools, playgroups and youth clubs, present an 'infrastructure of childhood'. They offer opportunities for library provision but require special attention to ensure effective liaison and community involvement. Today's children are the library's future.

2.2.2 The needs of individual children

Whatever the age or ability of the child, an experience of literature, whether fiction or non-fiction, and of other library materials, is recognized as being of great benefit to child development. It plays a formative role at a time when children's mental boundaries are not yet fixed.

Five areas of child development demonstrate the need for library materials:

- *intellectual and emotional development* (books and stories have a significant contribution here)
- *language development*, which is particularly crucial in the pre-school years (an area where the library can enhance the partnership between parent, child and teacher)
- *social development* (children's attitudes to one another and to society are significantly shaped by reading)
- *educational development* (the need for children to acquire reading and information skills is reinforced throughout the National Curriculum)
- *motor skills development* (books, toys and games can contribute to motor coordination).

2.3   The child and the library

The value of public libraries to children lies both in the materials provided, and in the means of provision. Library materials offer:

- *enjoyment* of the story experience, of language and of associated art
- *knowledge* of the wider world through both fiction and non-fiction
- *understanding* of other people, their behaviour, cultures, situations
- *self-knowledge*, identity (both individual and cultural) and security
- *information*, through both problem-solving and unguided discovery
- *confidence* in the acquisition of vocabulary, speech and language skills
- *shared experiences* between adult and child
- *support* for both formal and informal education.

Libraries additionally offer:

- *assistance*, guidance, interpretation, enthusiasm and encouragement from trained staff
- *a wider range* of materials than home or school can generally provide
- *resources* for every child, regardless of background and culture
- *access* to locally based services at a choice of times and places
- *free loan* and use of the majority of materials
- *a gateway* to the greater library network
- *neutral ground* between home and school for independent and unhindered discovery
- *skills development* in information handling
- *experience* of the library as an inviting and social place, with activities and events
- *community facilities* that have potential lifelong relevance
- *objective* information
- *literacy* support.

2.4   Service philosophy

2.4.1   The user

The library's responsibility is to the local child population as a whole, not just its current users. Every child is a potential user, and all children should be reached in some way. This will involve working directly with children, and also through a variety of agencies working with children.

The authority should consider the child rather than the organization when determining the nature of services. Children from all backgrounds and cultures have an equal right of access to library services. These services should in turn reflect and respect the background and culture of every child. Positive action is needed to do this and not simply provision of materials. Children with special needs require provision appropriate to these needs.

2.4.2 The overall service

Work with children is an integral part of the whole range of public library services. Overall policy, aims and objectives, and in particular staffing and training policies, must reflect this. Barriers between adult and children's services should be minimized, both publicly and administratively, to create a continuum of service to individuals.

All service providers, particularly of specialist services such as reference, local studies, music and drama, must agree a consistent and positive policy for child users and must be aware of the child dimension in any changes or developments in provision.

There should be clearly defined relationships between service providers, and these should be explicitly stated in an integrated strategy. See Recommendation 1 in *Investing in children*.[1]

Given the nature of the client group, posts with specialist knowledge, training and experience have an important part to play in the delivery of library services.

2.4.3 Service delivery

The children's service requires:

- an integrated strategy
- clear and deliverable aims and objectives
- an overall service policy statement, including
  - a planning and design policy
  - a staffing policy
  - a training policy
  - a stock policy (including selection)
  - a finance policy
  - an IT policy
  - a promotion and activities policy
- clear standards
- a monitoring system for evaluation and performance
- a public expression of aims and standards with an opportunity for feedback.

References

1 Library and Information Services Council (England), *Investing in children*, (DNH Library Information Series No. 22), HMSO, 1995.

3 Service entitlement

3.1 Introduction

A service must be clear about what the children in the community are entitled to and how they are going to access it. The overall purpose, aims and objectives need to be identified, and equality of access needs to be assured for all. This includes

- access for specific client groups (under-fives and young people, and those with special needs)
- access to literacy and information skills
- consultation with children so that they are involved with the local democratic process and with decision making on provision to meet their needs.

3.2 Mission, aims and objectives

The purpose of the children's service should be identified and made public to users. While mission statements vary between services, they usually cover access, development of skills and a love of reading. Here are some examples:

> We exist to develop enquiring minds, encourage a love of reading and stimulate the imagination of young people, ensuring that libraries are for life.[1]

> [To ensure that] every child in Nottinghamshire will grow up valuing books and reading as a source of pleasure and information and will take the fullest advantage of the public library service to enhance their lives and help them fulfil their potential.[2]

> The service is founded on the firm belief that libraries make a major contribution to children's and young people's development and can help them achieve their full potential. Their quality of life and learning can be significantly enhanced through ideas and information contained in books and other media. The needs of children and young people are at the heart of the library service. The goal is to provide a high quality service for all children and young people in North Tyneside, regardless of gender, disability, ethnic, cultural or religious background.[3]

Overall aims and objectives should cover the following areas:

- promotion of literacy and love of reading
- motivation to use and enjoy books as part of children's natural development
- provision of a wide range of resources to support lifelong learning and self development
- helping and supporting parents and carers
- information provision
- creation of an attractive, lively and welcoming environment
- activities and promotional events
- helping individuals and groups gain skills and confidence in using libraries and all types of materials
- stimulating community development through partnership working with other agencies.

3.3   General children's service strategy

3.3.1 Aim

The overall aim is to provide all children, their parents and carers with a high quality library service that is readily and easily available to them.

3.3.2 Objectives

These should be:

- to develop the skill of reading by providing stock which is appropriate for acquiring and developing this skill;
- to encourage reading for pleasure and enjoyment;
- to develop activities with a sense of purpose which promote the library and reflect the overall service objectives;
- to ensure sufficient resources to support the homework and leisure needs of children;
- to provide access to technology such as software, CD-ROMs and the Internet;
- to train staff in listening and enquiry skills so that children have the best opportunity of finding what they want;
- to develop information handling skills.

3.4   Under-fives

For children in the pre-school age group (roughly 0 to 5) the public library provides the only library service to which they are entitled by right, and consideration of their needs must take into account the needs of parents and carers also.[4]

Under-fives are dependent on their parents or carers for access to the library, and vary more than other groups in their experiences, opportunities and external stimuli.

3.4.1 Aims

The stated aims (in addition to the overall aim given above) are:

- to promote the role of books and stories in the development of the imagination, of language and literacy, and of emotional development
- to raise the awareness of libraries amongst those involved in the care of very young children
- to realize the potential of serving the two audiences – children and their carers – by promoting awareness of other relevant areas of library and information services
- to attempt to overcome the isolation of many parents/carers of young children by taking the service out to the potential users.

3.4.2 Objectives

The objectives should be:

- to provide an attractive library environment
- to provide stock and activities to foster a love and enthusiasm for reading

- to initiate a lifelong habit of library use
- to develop an integrated approach to work with this age group by liaising with other local authority departments, specialist agencies, voluntary organizations etc.

3.4.3 Entitlements for under-fives

In Birmingham this has been formulated into a series of entitlements. The full range of entitlements are varied according to the size of each library and the facilities available. The Centre for the Child, opened in Birmingham Central Library in 1995, brings together library facilities for children, teenage provision, meeting rooms, and a parents' information service – along with a high level of provision for disabled children, and for under-fives. Its under-fives entitlement reads:

We have

- trained staff who will respond to you and your child with care and understanding
- staff who can show you where to find the appropriate books for your child at different ages and recommend suitable books for your child
- a wide choice of books, including books which reflect lifestyles, cultures and languages
- information about under fives groups in the area
- a Parent and Child room with changing facilities available
- toilets for under fives to use
- a playpen, and toys for under fives to play with in the library.

You are welcome to breastfeed your baby here.[5]

3.5   Young people

3.5.1 Aim

In addition to the general aim stated above, the aim is to provide and promote a wide range of quality resources to meet both the short and longer-term information and leisure needs of young people.

3.5.2 Objectives

The additional objectives should be:

- to provide a transition from children's services to adult services
- to encourage lifelong use of the library for learning purposes
- to promote lifelong reading for information and pleasure
- to provide skills for information literacy
- to provide library collections and services for all young people in the community to meet educational, information, cultural and leisure needs.

It is important that the services for young people should be designed not only by librarians but in cooperation with the target group, whose choices could be different from what libraries traditionally offer. It is our responsibility to respect these different needs and provide the opportunity for choice. This means providing stock to suit young people's needs and wants, presenting it in a way to stimulate their interest, and encouraging them by making them feel welcome.

3.6   Special needs

In recent years children with special needs have been integrated into mainstream services whenever possible. Public library services should aim to meet the needs of all children, covering the wide range of abilities including the needs of disabled children, and regardless of gender, social class and ethnic or cultural background. In order to achieve equality of access for all, consideration needs to be given to the types of services available and how they are promoted, as well as to how buildings and resources may be adapted.

Library authorities should make provision for children experiencing:

- specific language/cultural needs (e.g. ethnic communities, traveller children)
- geographical isolation (e.g. rural communities or those without public transport)
- financial disadvantage (e.g. many lone parent families)
- educational disadvantage (e.g. where parents/carers have limited literacy skills)
- problems associated with gifted children
- behavioural and social difficulties (e.g. inability to mix with other children)
- learning disabilities
- physical disabilities.

The Disability Discrimination Act 1995[6] makes it unlawful for people who provide goods and services to the public to discriminate against disabled people. Libraries are included in the scope of the legislation, which will be implemented progressively between 1996 and 2002. More detailed advice will be available during this period but it is clear that libraries will need to 'take reasonable steps' to change policies, practices and procedures and may have to make adjustments to library buildings and/or offer the service in alternative ways. The Library Association's *Can everybody reach you? Improving library services for blind and partially sighted people*[7] is a useful starting point when considering access issues.

3.6.1 Auditing and improving services

The following measures are recommended:

- ensuring that the community profile includes the number of children with special needs
- investigating the languages spoken in the catchment area and including them in the profile
- assessing and evaluating what is already being provided
- carrying out an access audit covering buildings and publicity
- introducing an integrated strategy (see 5.3)
- seeking specialist advice, especially on building adaptations, either from within the authority or from organizations linked with the authority.

3.6.2 What else can be done?

Other desirable measures might include:

- provision of interpreters for the hearing impaired, to accompany storytelling sessions
- provision of Kurzweil reading machines for the visually impaired
- provision of appropriate technologies such as multimedia PCs to broaden access
- visits by the mobile library to children on traveller sites
- installation and use of induction loops
- promotion of interactive group work
- dual-language storytelling.

3.7 Children's charters

Some authorities are expressing their aims and objectives in the form of a charter for services for children, which they display clearly in the library and distribute by means of bookmarks, or leaflets. Here is an example of such a charter:

We promise

- to *listen* to what you have to say about your library
- to *explain* how the library works and how to use it
- to *help* you find the books and information you need
- to *provide* the best books and other resources for you to enjoy
- to *encourage* you to read as widely and as often as possible
- to *encourage* you to take part in imaginative activities.

We will do our best to make your library a

- safe
- attractive
- friendly

place for you and your family to visit.[8]

Alternatively some authorities are producing authority-wide charters for children covering all services. This has been the result of partnership working, and the development of an integrated strategy following the implementation of The Children Act 1989[9] and subsequent legislation.

3.8 Literacy

The library service has a key role in fostering literacy. It can exercise this in three ways:

- by providing and promoting material which assists reading development in young children
- by organizing activities (sometimes with other agencies) which promote literacy
- by providing and promoting services which assist those with literacy difficulties.

3.8.1 Material for reading development

Literacy begins with language development, and language begins for young children through interaction with a caring adult. All of a library's book stock is therefore relevant, but material for the very young is especially critical. Experience of nursery rhymes, finger games, board books and other simple stories is fundamental, both in laying the foundations for successful literacy, and in pre-empting later literacy difficulties. This should be emphasized when library services for the very young are promoted to parents and carers. Parents may be discouraged by charges or by complicated regulations and procedures. Libraries should ensure:

- that there is no lower age limit below which children are refused access to books
- that fines and charges are removed, or at least minimized
- that forms are easy to read and straightforward to complete.

Provision of material to help with the early stages of learning to read is essential. Libraries should therefore ensure:

- that they have an attractive range of first reading material
- that the signing and promotion of such material does not discourage older children who may still need to use it
- that they have a policy in respect of graded reading schemes
- that they are aware of literacy levels in different catchment areas, and of local schools' approaches to the teaching of reading
- that assistance is offered to parents and carers who may be choosing such material for their children.

Adults should be provided with resources and information about helping children develop reading skills.

3.8.2 Organizing activities to promote literacy

Most library activities will in some way foster literacy, or provide a model for parents to emulate. Storytelling, or simply sharing stories together, is not only enjoyable for children, but enables the library service to prompt parents to make time for this activity themselves.

Reading games, holiday events and other promotions can provide assistance with literacy. Consideration should be given to involving children throughout the range of reading abilities.

Library services should be promoted to parents and carers of babies. Birmingham Libraries Bookstart initiative, begun in 1992, involved both library staff and health visitors, who presented packs of material to new parents when their child reached nine months old. Items such as a free book, library joining card, booklists, and other leaflets were included, and parents were invited to share books with their young child. Research reports[10] on the children's subsequent progress have been very encouraging, and the scheme has since been emulated by many other library services under different titles. Such schemes provide useful models for this type of promotion.

Libraries should initiate and support collaborative approaches to literacy with other local authority departments, notably education, social services, the voluntary sector and other providers, such as lifelong learning initiatives and family literacy initiatives.

3.8.3 Services for those with literacy difficulties

Material should be provided, throughout the age range, for those children whose reading age lags behind that of their contemporaries. This is particularly important with older children, where its promotion needs to be careful and tactful.

There should be collaboration between adult and children's services with regard to material for young people with reading difficulties. Literacy difficulties should be borne in mind in areas such as:

- signs and location guides, which should be in clear, readable print
- promotional literature, which should be in plain English
- translations into community languages
- computer facilities, whose instructions and screen layouts should be adapted to suit a range of literacy levels
- enrolment and reservation forms, which should be easy to follow.

3.9   Consulting children

To be effective, the library service needs to know the views and wants of children, and to use these in the planning and development of services. Seeking their opinions enables the service:

- to encourage children to build a role in society
- to listen to what children have to say
- to ensure the library service is appropriate and responsive
- to build working relationships
- to develop communication, observation and listening skills in children.

There are several different issues which must be considered.

3.9.1 The Children Act 1989

The Act requires that consultation with under-eights must be carefully publicized through schools, the media and bookmarks, etc., for children to take home. No one-to-one interviews should be conducted in isolated venues and all participating staff must wear clear identification.[11]

3.9.2 Whose views are being expressed?

Written questionnaires and parent-and-child sessions tend to elicit parents' views. Questions asked at school often produce the answers that children think are required of them. Group discussions tend to reflect the group culture.

3.9.3 What age group?

The service needs to find appropriate ways of communicating with, for example, very young children to enable them to influence development. Questionnaires, interviews and quizzes need to be jargon-free and to be carried out by staff who can communicate well with children (who often know what they want and have something valuable to say), and can deal with the information gained.

3.9.4 What types of surveying are possible?

The possibilities include:

- questionnaires
- interviews
- unobtrusive testing
- focus groups
- observation
- group discussion
- Video Box
- quizzes.

3.9.5 What is the base information required?

The national children's library survey, currently being piloted by CIPFA (the Chartered Institute of Public Finance and Accountancy), is built around questions such as:

- Why have you come to the library?
- How many items have you borrowed?
- What were you looking for?
- What information do you need?
- How often do you visit?
- How old are you?
- Are you a girl or a boy?
- What do you think of libraries?
- Who do you come with?
- What do you like about libraries?
- What would make them better?

References

1 Hertfordshire Libraries, Arts and Information Services, 1994.

2 *Service specification: Children and young people*, Nottinghamshire County Library Service, 1996.

3 North Tyneside Libraries (Children and Young People's Statement), 1995.

4 Library and Information Services Council (England), *Investing in children*, (DNH Library Information Series, No. 22), HMSO, 1995.

5 Birmingham Libraries, Department of Leisure and Community Services, *Welcome to children under five (service entitlement)*, Birmingham Libraries, 1996.

6 Great Britain, Statutes, *Disability Discrimination Act*, Ch. 50, HMSO, 1995.

7 Library Association (in association with the RNIB), *Can everybody reach you? Improving library services for blind and partially sighted people* (Guidance Note), Library Association, 1993.

8 This Charter was devised by The South Eastern Education and Library Board (Northern Ireland)'s Library and Information Service in 1993.

9 Great Britain, Statutes, *The Children Act*, Ch. 41, HMSO, 1989.

10 Wade, B. and Moore, M., *Bookstart in Birmingham* (Book Trust Report No. 2), Book Trust, 1993.

11 Great Britain, Statutes, *The Children Act*, Ch. 41, HMSO, 1989, op. cit.

4 Specifying the service

4.1 Introduction

The aim of a specification is to provide a realistic statement quantifying the standards and targets of service delivery that a child can expect from any library. The library profile will provide an assessment of a particular library against the specification and targets for service improvement.

How a service specification is created will depend on whether it is to become part of a specification for the whole service, or whether it is to stand alone. The issues to be included are the same, but the approach may be completely different. If the authority is producing an overall specification it is important that where possible the children's issues are fully integrated. This will ensure that the necessary chapter on specific issues is kept short and focused on key children's issues.

The specification needs to be built around the service priorities and the management information and data available. This chapter does no more than ask questions, as there is no simple solution that can be applied to all cases.

4.2 Standards and targets

What is the specification trying to achieve? The specification should set standards for service provision and should make it clear whether these are to be minimum, maximum or current standards. It may include a service target to improve on this standard.

There should be provision for each library to assess its service against the standard, to add local circumstances which may affect performance, and to set targets in order to reach that standard. This constitutes the *library profile*. Finally, the target-setting, monitoring and evaluation process should be agreed.

When creating a specification you must ensure:

- that standards or targets can be measured relatively easily
- that information is only collected which can then be used to improve provision
- that the staff understand why a standard is important and how it impacts on development
- that the staff understand how much weight should be given to local circumstances when setting the local library profile
- that standards are compatible.

4.3 Potential standards

Before starting to decide what standards the service wishes to achieve, it is important to consider what is achievable. Let us now consider the key issues to be included in a service specification.

4.3.1 Buildings and environment

The following points need to be considered:

- *safety* to ensure the particular needs of children are taken into account
- *space*
    - the proportion of space available for the children's library (20%)
    - ease of circulation for a double buggy, electric scooter or wheelchair
    - space within the library for young people's material
- *security*, a safe and secure environment with good oversight
- *layout*, shelves and stock at an appropriate height for the user
- *furniture and equipment* appropriate to user needs and including IT
- *signs and guiding* that are clear and easy to read.

4.3.2 Community profile

The first requirement is an understanding of the community served, including:

- a breakdown of potential users in appropriate age categories
- the number and type of groups, schools and agencies
- the languages spoken
- special needs analysis.

Take-up by the population should be recorded, including:

- what percentage of the child population are registered borrowers
- what percentage of active borrowers are children
- what percentage of the registered borrowers are children
- what percentage of service users are children (to be assessed by survey).

Other matters for consideration are:

- services available which are either free or for which a charge is made
- systems to enable children to comment on library services
- consultation processes for children.

4.3.3 Stock

Stock is a key element of service provision, and adequate management data is important to ensure that the stock available is used to its maximum potential. Most automated systems can give data if set up to do so. However, children's stock and loans figures have often been combined or included with adult figures. Senior managers should request the creation of adequate management data to enable them to target service delivery.

There are four main sections to the stock specification: stock available, stock usage, age of stock, and budget. It is important that all sections have clear measurable standards and that clear targets are set instead of using phrases like 'small proportion/percentage' or 'a collection of'.

Stock available

The first criterion is the overall stock per head of child population. Under-fives have only one section so it is good practice to calculate relevant stock per head of under-fives. A total stock target should be used with caution, as it may result in unnecessary retention of dated books or ones in poor condition.

The categories of stock that a library must provide should be identified (e.g. younger readers). Each category should then be quantified as a proportion of the whole children's stock.

The demand and use of libraries varies with size, so where an authority has libraries of different sizes it is recommended that they are grouped according to size and that stock targets are related to these groupings. It should be noted that the profile of children's stock targets by size of library will be different from those set for the adult libraries.

Usage

There is a need to specify the expected average turnover per section or category of stock.

Age of stock

An age profile for stock, i.e. the average shelf life, should be set and measured (e.g. paperback three years).

Budget

The LISC report *Investing in children* notes in recommendation 8:

> The percentage of the total materials budget applied to services for children and young people should be determined locally and should be at least the same as the percentage of children and young people in the population served. The percentage should be determined and should be subject to regular review.[1]

This should ensure that children get their fair share of resources, and budget decisions should take into consideration usage, wear and tear, and average cost of items.

The specification should recommend how the library should profile this budget against categories to ensure stock levels are maintained. This is where the local targets will vary from the standard.

Other factors

Flexibility needs to be built into this process as new categories are added. It can take two or more years' extensive spending to increase a category by 1% of the overall stock depending on the size of the category. Other useful stock standards include:

- additions to stock
- physical condition of stock
- circulating collections
- requests from children.

4.3.4 Staff

There is a need to specify the staffing needs of children's sections, plus the staff training opportunities available in children's work.

4.3.5 Information services

Standards for dealing with children's enquiries should be the same as those for adults, and should cover:

- how enquiries can be made
- ways to encourage youngsters to develop information handling skills
- use of IT
- response times
- accuracy and level of help
- referrals.

4.3.6 Services to schools, playgroups and other organizations

The specification should take into account:

- the separate roles of the public library service and schools library service (where there is one)
- the groups that each library service can serve including levels, frequency and loan arrangements
- special service arrangements which can be made for certain individuals or groups (e.g. childminders, special needs groups).

4.3.7 Promotion of literacy and libraries

It is useful to have a statement indicating the purpose of activities for children in order to promote reading and the use of the library. The statement should note that they are to be organized and staffed in accordance with the Children Act 1989. The LA guidance note *Unsupervised children in libraries*[2] is also a valuable reference tool. Items for inclusion are:

- storytimes (giving frequency, length, required size of audience and evaluation process)
- other activities, quantified by size of library and audience size
- authority-wide activities, giving the required standard for involvement.
- staff talks and presentations.

4.3.8 Mobile library services

Standards for children's provision on a mobile or trailer library service should be indicated. It is particularly valuable to compare borrower statistics with stock proportions, as the children's section is often inadequate on a mobile. A flexible approach to the stocking of mobiles is important to cover seasonal variations and different communities.

4.3.9 Publicity

There is a need to specify the quantity, level and graphic requirements of publicity for children.

4.4 Monitoring and evaluating

It must be clear from the start how the specification is to be monitored. It takes time to set up library profiles for all libraries within an authority but once established the monitoring system can be quite straightforward.

Monitoring can be carried out by any one or a combination of the following:

- the head of the library service
- the head of children's services
- staff with responsibility for working with children in each library or group of libraries
- children's peer groups.

The following will be required to monitor the profiles against standards:

- personal visits
- direct observation
- analysis of data
- collection of statistics
- discussions with staff
- survey of children's opinions
- analysis of comments and complaints
- unobtrusive testing
- comparison with other like authorities
- benchmarking.

Data must be collected from the outset by the most appropriate people, so as to ensure that no gaps are found at the end of the review period.

It is also important that the specification and standards themselves are rigorously examined. This will ensure that the information collected is used and that the standards are still appropriate to service provision.

References

1 Library and Information Services Council (England), *Investing in children*, (DNH Library Information Series No. 22), HMSO, 1995.
2 Library Association, *Unsupervised children in libraries* (Guidance Note), Library Association, 1991.

5 Relationships between service providers

5.1 Introduction

The introduction of Local Management of Schools (LMS in England and Wales and DMR in Scotland) has resulted in the identification and definition of the relationships between public libraries, schools library services and school libraries. LMS, together with the emergence of a grant-maintained sector and the delegation of budgets to schools, has produced a varied pattern of provision throughout England and Wales. This has the following consequences:

- It is essential that schools library services establish a clear agreement with the public library service on their respective roles.
- Local authorities need to develop integrated strategies for the delivery of library and information services for children, in order to support the needs of the curriculum, and broader educational needs both in and out of school.
- Library services for children need to be on the corporate agenda. Support from chief executive and chief officers will make the development of an integrated strategy much easier.

In this section we have assumed services will be provided to all schools, whether grant maintained, independent or local authority. Where this is not the case their needs must not be overlooked.

5.2 Roles and responsibilities

The LISC Report *Investing in children* notes that:

> The public library service in general is not adequately resourced to make up for the deficiencies of educational institutions . . . nor does it have professional specialist staff in sufficient numbers to cope with the additional demands from pupils . . . [1]

Good communication between schools library service staff and public library staff is essential to enable maximum benefit from such contacts. Public libraries can provide the following for children, parents, carers and teachers:

- books and other materials for individual use
- individual library membership
- information and reference material for use in the library, and in a variety of media
- advice/talks to parents and carers about books and reading development
- class visits to the library to help children develop the habit of reading and library use, and an opportunity for them to learn how to use library resources
- visits by authors, illustrators and storytellers to public libraries to foster children's enjoyment of reading and books
- visits to schools to promote public library use
- provision in the children's library of books about reading and child care for parents and carers
- encouragement and support of reading for pleasure.

The following should be primarily the responsibility of schools library services:

- bulk loans/project loans issued in the name of the school
- special loan facilities and professional material on reading for teachers
- advice on school library organiziation and management
- advice/talks on books and other media related to curriculum topics or themes
- in-service training for teachers
- advice to governors, teachers and school librarians on school library policy and development
- pre/post-OFSTED inspection guidance and support
- curriculum-related talks, and professional advice and support to school librarians
- help in organizing school-based book promotions (e.g. book fairs)
- creation of curriculum-related booklists, advisory documents etc.
- guidance on IT developments
- book-purchase schemes
- advice to LEA officers and elected members
- involvement in curriculum development
- advice and support on independent and resource-based learning.

The following should be primarily the responsibility of school libraries themselves:

- a central location for the majority of the school's learning resources, and ensuring that it is professionally managed
- wide-ranging and accessible collections of resources in a variety of media, technologies and formats to support the curriculum
- work space for whole classes, small groups and individuals engaged in study
- information to pupils and teachers on library-based and external resources
- a 'learning laboratory' to develop progressively independent study, literacy and information handling skills
- supporting the efforts of teachers and parents in developing pupils' skills as efficient readers
- managing staff collections
- encouraging and supporting pupils' reading for pleasure
- promotion of the school library as an effective learning environment
- involvement in curriculum development in conjunction with subject departments
- acting as an important resource in school for leisure and recreational needs.

5.3 Integrated strategies

When developing integrated strategies, it is recommended that local authorities concentrate in the first instance on the three principal channels of service delivery:

- public library service
- schools library service
- school libraries.

The key elements in a strategy should focus on the following issues:

- children's needs with respect to books, libraries, information and the encouragement of reading
- the specific roles and responsibilities of the key partners in meeting these needs
- the advantages and benefits to be gained by all the partners from a considered and carefully implemented strategy, particularly with regard to value for money, avoidance of wasteful duplication and guarding against major needs being missed altogether
- coordination, collaboration and joint or cross-agency initiatives.

Strategies should be supported by local examples of service initiatives and good practice, and checklists for service provision. Consideration should be given to variations in need.

To be effective, such strategies will need the endorsement of appropriate local authority committees, head teachers and governing bodies, and the support of staff in those library services which are party to such strategies.

From this it may be possible to expand the coverage of the strategy to include joint working and partnerships with a range of other providers such as social services, education, health, youth and other external agencies. These are referred to later in the *Guidelines*.

5.4 Structures

A number of alternative structures for schools library services have resulted from LMS and local authority decisions about the directorates in which libraries should be placed. These range from direct management by the local education authority to the creation of free-standing business units. However, change is not simply about structure, and many services have had to develop new ways of working in the emerging climate of 'competition'. Integrated and separate service provision both have certain advantages.

5.4.1 Integrated public library and education library service provision

- This leads to a more coordinated approach towards service development, promotion and delivery, as children's needs can be identified and met on a broader front than just the public library.
- It offers a more cost-effective means of service delivery in terms of shared access to facilities such as approval collections, bibliographical support, vehicles and premises, and shared knowledge about the particular needs of the children.
- It gives greater flexibility in the use of staffing.

5.4.2 Separate public library and education library service provision

- This avoids the split line-management responsibility imposed on staff at senior level and (depending upon structures), at middle management level as well. Being responsible to two managers can lead to conflicting service demands, loyalties and priorities.

- The distinct roles and responsibilities of each arm of the service, can be clearly defined by means of statements of policy, business objectives and functions.
- There is less danger of one arm of provision gaining prominence over the other.

5.4.3 Working with other departments in an emergency

There needs to be a clearly defined and deliverable role for the children's library service as part of a local authority's emergency plans. The main objective will be to provide information for children. However, storytelling and activities may be the first step an authority requires in an emergency, to help calm the children and to occupy them while parents and carers come to terms with the situation and make decisions.

References

1 Library and Information Services Council (England), *Investing in children*, (DNH Library Information Series No. 22), HMSO, 1995.

6 Library design and layout planning

6.1 Introduction

The siting, layout and design of children's libraries is an important part of library provision. Upon the creation of a library and any subsequent refurbishment it is important to review these issues to develop provision. The special features and particular needs of the client group must be taken into account, and a senior member of staff experienced in library work with children should be involved in the planning process. Before starting the planning process it is important to develop a clear vision of what is to be achieved.

6.2 Location within the library building

6.2.1 Key issues

When deciding on the location the following issues need to be considered:

- an easily accessible ground floor location (stairs can constitute a psychological barrier as well as a serious obstacle on health and convenience grounds, such as for children in wheelchairs, parents with pushchairs, and elderly people with grandchildren)
- the need for adequate supervision for both safety and security
- the desirability of a safe, yet prominent, position
- the best way to cater for young people (options include a separate room, a separate section of stock, or integration into the main sequence; provision must be closely linked with adult facilities)
- the desired relationship between the children's library and the adult library.

6.2.2 Separate or shared provision?

Consideration of the key issues on location usually results in one of these two options. Separate rooms for both adults and children offer potential advantages:

- a clearly defined area for children (an important psychological factor in terms of atmosphere, behaviour, 'ownership' and security)
- a designated space for activities
- an opportunity for flexibility in deciding acceptable noise levels.

An open-plan area for shared use affords the following benefits:

- recognition of the family as a unit
- ease of transition from child to adult use of facilities
- ease of access to (and promotion of) stock
- wider staff involvement in work with children
- cost-effective use of space, resources and staffing.

6.3 Dual use

The provision of dual-use facilities (i.e. shared school and library provision) is an option that can be considered. They must be well sited and should be perceived to be an integral part of the community. They require the full cooperation of the school and its staff, and of the public library service, but can offer a number of advantages to both:

- by combining resources, both school and public library are able to offer a greater range of material than they might otherwise provide.
- there is the opportunity to share staffing resources.
- there is a potential opportunity for longer opening hours for both sets of users.
- shared resources avoid wasteful duplication.

The problems to consider in such provision are:

- the difference in emphasis between the school and public library service, and how that could be catered for
- potential conflict as a result of large-scale use by school children and the public at the same time
- times when library use may have to be restricted to only one category of users
- ownership of assets and payment for the provision of facilities such as IT
- access for children in school holidays.

6.4 Space

When defining the space requirements for the children's area it will be necessary to consider:

- allocating an area that corresponds to the proportion of children in the local population (usually 20% of the space)
- how much space is needed to manoeuvre wheelchairs, electric scooters and double buggies esily
- the extra floor space required for shelving that children can reach
- the need for a high percentage of face-on display of stock
- shelving for a large proportion of paperback stock
- extra space for the display of two and three dimensional materials
- computer hardware
- the recommendations in *Standards for public libraries*[1] which stipulate 16m^2 for every 1000 volumes on the open shelves
- a separate area for the under-fives
- a parents' collection
- children's activities
- provision of homework/study facilities (possibly a homework centre)
- provision of toilets and/or handbasins and/or baby care facilities
- storage.

6.5 Electrics

The space should conform to the latest standards for electrical equipment and there should be a regular plan of equipment testing. To cope with advancements in technology new buildings should be flood-wired. Older buildings should be upgraded to provide adequate IT cabling, phone lines, TV aerial and CCTV cabling and lighting levels. An induction loop should also be included.

6.6 Furniture

The furniture used in children's libraries should be safe, sturdy and of good quality, and should support equality of access. Colourful and imaginative design should be sought. If the products of different manufacturers are used, it is important that they should complement each other. Libraries attract children from a wide age range, for whom atmosphere and look are important, and whose tastes change relatively rapidly. Design features will need to appeal to all but will also need to remain in fashion.

6.6.1 General shelving issues

The stock capacity must be based on client-related criteria. From the total stock figure, a shelf stock figure should be calculated (i.e. number of items on open access and available for use at any one time by children). From this, in turn, the balance of stock between different age groups and formats can be determined.

The height of the shelving must relate to the age of the children using the stock, and should not normally be above 1200mm for island shelving and 1500mm for wall-mounted shelving. As far as practicable, upper and lower shelf heights should allow for use by children with special physical needs.

Sloping display shelves should be used extensively, particularly in the area for younger children. Where possible, shelves which can be easily converted from flat to display should be used. Initial purchase of additional shelving will ensure maximum flexibility in meeting the future needs of customers.

The use of wheel-lockable mobile shelving could be considered but loading should also be considered if regular movement of the shelves is required.

6.6.2 Stock issues

- *Picture books* should be displayed so as to make full use of attractive cover designs, either in kinderboxes or in other browser boxes, and on sloping display shelves. Kinderboxes are now available in a range of colourful designs, which combine facilities for imaginative play, storage and seating (e.g. train, animal, cube and other shapes). Where large-format picture books are provided, appropriate display and storage are also necessary.
- *Paperbacks* are best displayed in face-out form to maximize the appeal of attractive jacket designs, or else integrated with the hardback stock for more purposeful selection. Options include sloping shelves, paperback units within shelving systems, tiered shelving, zigzags and separate stands, dump bins etc.
- *Shelving for cassettes, videos and computer software* needs to strike an acceptable balance between accessibility and security.
- *Toys and games* could be stored in some form of box or bin which provides maximum flexibility.

6.6.3 Other issues

- Where there is a counter in the children's library, its height must be appropriate to child users.
- Every effort should be made to provide an enquiry desk or enquiry point. This should be staffed as frequently as possible, and at least at peak hours of use.
- In all but the smallest library, some study facility should be provided. As well as seating for study, consideration should also be given to providing low coffee tables, easy chairs, bean bags or other informal seating, and stacking chairs for activities. Consideration should be given to children in wheelchairs. It is worth having at least one table which is height-adjustable.
- Display facilities, notice boards and display cases for three-dimensional material should be included.
- Blackout facilities should be provided in order to broaden the range of activities available.
- Children's and young people's libraries should be clearly signed throughout the building, and guiding within stock areas should be highly visible. Shelf guides and a plan of the library should be provided, and tactile signs should be considered. The language used for guiding should be client-orientated; lower-case lettering should be used except for the initial letter, and Dewey classification included on shelf and bay guiding. An explanation of Dewey is also recommended.
- A catalogue or other access terminal should be provided where possible, and a subject index is essential. Where the catalogue is computerized, the language and method of operation should be user-friendly.
- The whole area occupied by the children's library should be carpeted (though activity areas may include vinyl flooring for painting etc.).
- All furniture and equipment should be regularly checked to ensure that there are no sharp or dangerous edges or surfaces. Electrical equipment needs to be checked for tamper-proof plugs and socket covers.
- Baby care facilities should be provided.

6.7 Safety features

These are vital in planning and should cover the following:

- security of children in an environment which brings children into close contact with adults
- lockable castors on mobile shelving and trolleys
- firmly fixed wall shelving and well-braced island shelving
- space for wheelchairs, electric scooters and double buggies to circulate
- paperback stands with a firm base that are stable even when only half full
- kinderboxes with rounded corners and no design pieces sticking out
- electric sockets to be covered with safety plugs and covers
- good visibility for staff and carers including CCTV facilities
- alarms to be installed in toilet and baby-changing facilities
- all glass items to be reinforced according to health and safety requirements

- fire alarms to be fitted with flashing lights as well as sound
- fire-retardant material and non-toxic fittings to be used
- automatic doors to be activated at a height which does not allow toddlers to leave unaccompanied
- upstairs windows to be fitted with safety catches
- under-fives areas to be sited furthest away from exits
- posters alerting parents and carers to their responsibilities regarding the safety of their children
- safety guidelines for staff alerting them to their legal and moral responsibilities
- door closures to have slow-return hinges, and where possible a finger gap to be left between doors when closed.

6.8 The adult library

In order to ensure continuity for children using adult library areas (both intermittently, for study purposes, and permanently, as they reach adulthood), planning and design decisions should be coordinated. This particularly applies to issues such as:

- young people's provision within the adult library
- guiding that follows a consistent style
- sufficient study facilities in the adult library
- counter heights when they are to be shared by adults and children.

6.9 Consultation

With a new library or refurbishment, or when developing young people's provision, consultation is valuable. Options include focus groups, fliers, open meetings or comments boards for local children, for carers and for specialist organizations or groups in the area. Their purpose is to obtain the views of those who will ultimately use the new facilities, to encourage ownership, to ensure the new library is effective in meeting the needs of the community, and to give specialist advice when and where you need it.

(For more detail on this subject Michael Dewe's *Planning and designing libraries for children and young people* is recommended.[2])

References

1 International Federation of Library Associations and Institutions (IFLA), *Standards for public libraries*, IFLA, 1973.
2 Dewe, Michael, *Planning and designing libraries for children and young people*, Library Association Publishing, 1995.

7 Staffing

7.1 Introduction

Staff are a vital resource and they must be deployed to deliver a targeted, relevant and high-quality service. This has major implications for the recruitment and selection of staff, staffing structures and levels, personnel issues and training.

The 1989 Children Act and subsequent legislation should be borne in mind, as it requires local authorities to review and publicize existing services to children. This may lead to a re-examination of priorities and organization in libraries and may create further partnership opportunities with social services and education.

7.2 Knowledge and skills

The following skills must be present among the staffing resources of every authority in proportion to the client group:

- an understanding of child development, including intellectual, emotional, physical, behavioural, language and social development
- a detailed knowledge of children's books, IT hardware and software, AV multimedia etc.
- a knowledge of appropriate information resources and an ability to assess them
- a knowledge of educational trends, developments, terminology and local structures/patterns of organization
- a knowledge of child-related groups and organizations (i.e. schools, under-fives groups, youth clubs etc.), and an ability to work with them
- a familiarity with contemporary children's culture
- storytelling and other performance skills
- public speaking skills, particularly with regard to talking to groups of children, teachers, parents and carers
- teaching skills to promote effective library use
- promotional skills, particularly with regard to book promotion
- an understanding of parents' expectations and demands in relation to their children
- personal qualities, including empathy with children and confidence in relating with and to them
- management skills
- competence in working with IT
- cultural awareness and relevant language skills.

7.3 Implications for staffing policy

The required skills have the following implications for staffing policy:

- The library needs of children must be understood and acknowledged in all policy and decision-making areas, including the work of non-public departments.

- Children should have equality of opportunity with all other client groups as far as access to library provision and services are concerned.
- All staff should be trained (see 7.5).
- The detailed knowledge of child development, children's literature, IT software and networks, and educational matters, necessarily implies a specialist element within the staffing structure.
- Library assistants at public service points have the majority of contacts with individual children, and should be expected to develop knowledge of readers and an awareness of stock. They should not be expected to undertake professional work, but their invaluable role should be recognized.
- An appropriate recruitment and selection policy should exist whereby the library needs of children are recognized in all public library job descriptions and employee specifications. Note must also be taken of the requirements of The Rehabilitation of Offenders Act 1974.[1]
- Positive measures should be taken to recruit staff who reflect the make-up of the community.

7.4   Staffing structures

Authorities will differ in the ways in which they organize the management and delivery of services to children. Whatever staffing structure is chosen, however, it should evolve from broadly based professional discussion rather than from short-term or financial expediency. Two general principles apply:

- children's needs are important enough to require specialist posts
- children's needs are too important to be left just to specialist posts.

The following recommendations are made:

- The management of children's services requires a senior specialist post.
- This post should be on the service's senior management team (whether or not education services are combined in its responsibilities). The specialist's contribution at this level is not simply to represent the specialism but also implies involvement in collective policy-making and discussion.
- This post must be supported by a sufficient number of other specialist posts to enable full and consistent delivery of services to children. (This delivery includes training, development, whole-service initiatives, monitoring etc., in addition to the more visible activities at service points themselves.)
- The extent to which specialist posts extend through management (and/or geographically throughout the authority) will depend on the size and shape of the authority, the location of communities, the overall approach to staffing and the role of all other public services staff.
- All specialist posts should include a professional involvement in the wider context of the management and operation of the overall service, just as more generalist posts should include an understanding and ability to contribute to the specialist services.
- The responsibilities of other public service staff to children must be identified and

monitored, especially beyond the point at which specialist delivery of the service ends.

- All staff should be trained in work with children.

The provision of specialist and generalist posts at all levels must be considered, and attention needs to be focused on the detailed nature of the work to be undertaken. As was noted earlier, the provision of an effective library service to children requires staff with a range of skills, knowledge and expertise. When the actual staff posts are created it is suggested that a gradation of the specialism be undertaken. The matrix below gives an example of how this could be done. It is intended for completion by individual authorities, either as a training exercise or as a management process to clarify thinking.

Areas of Work (for key, see below)															
Post	1	2	3	4	5	6	7	8	9	10	11	12	13	14	15
Library Assistant															
Generalist Librarian															
Specialist Librarian															
Specialist senior Management Level															
Library Manager*															

Key contribution █████████   Light involvement ░░░░░░░░░

*Library manager i.e. a senior non librarian or administrator

Key
1   Library routines, e.g. shelving
2   Readers' advisory work with parents, children and carers
3   Storytelling, promotional activities
4   Visits to schools for liaison and planning work and to playgroups and other organized groups
5   Work with adult groups, i.e. talks on child development, books etc.
6   Stock management, e.g. selection
7   Class visits, explanation of services, book talks, information handling
8   Planning of work programmes
9   Budget management
10   Fund raising, e.g. sponsorship, income generation etc.
11   Responsibility for overall policy, resources, committee work, monitoring and evaluation and alignment of service provision
12   Liaison with the education and other departments of the local authority
13   Liaison with outside agencies
14   An authority-wide responsibility for coordinating, managing, developing and monitoring children's services

Notes

These areas of work are examples only. The list is not intended to be definitive but to indicate how a matrix could be devised using actual workloads.

Whatever mode of organization is adopted, it is strongly recommended that a specialist post should exist at a senior level within the structure.

Based on the required knowledge, skills and expertise identified earlier in this chapter, there is also a strong case to support the employment of specialists at a middle management level at the very least.

7.5 Training and development

Training of staff is vital and whilst no precise model can be drawn up which is applicable to every authority, certain key factors should be borne in mind:

- Whatever structure of staff organization exists, the training programme should ensure that the knowledge, skills and expertise (including IT skills) required to deliver a high quality library service to children are possessed in all staff to an appropriate degree.
- All staff, irrespective of seniority or specialist background, will benefit from having access to adequate and relevant training opportunities which will broaden their professional development.
- All staff should be made aware of the value the authority attaches to its public library provision for children.
- Training in work with children should form an integral part of both induction and cyclical training programmes for all levels of staff.
- Specialist and senior staff should receive training in management skills to broaden and further their professional development, and thus to increase the level of expertise present within the authority.
- Training provision needs to reflect the local authority's stated objectives in the delivery of library services to children. This provision should be carefully targeted and should be of a high standard in terms of both content and delivery.
- Training is an on-going process and should not be seen merely in terms of course provision. Every opportunity should therefore be taken, on a day-to-day basis, to develop and build on the commitment and expertise of staff at all levels.
- Any volunteers employed should be fully trained and arrangements should be on a proper contractual basis.
- Staff at all levels will benefit from access to coaching and workplace mentoring as part of staff development.
- Involvement of experts from other disciplines such as under-eights officers and youth workers in training will add an important dimension when dealing with specific client groups. Advantage should also be taken of other partnerships. For example, homework clubs might involve librarians, teachers, youth workers and parents.
- The Library Association's *Framework for continuing professional development* should be used.[2]

References

1 Great Britain, Statutes, *The Rehabilitation of Offenders Act*, Ch. 53, HMSO, 1974.
2 Library Association, *The framework for continuing professional development*, Library Association, 1992.

8 Stock

8.1 Introduction

When defining a stock policy the essential starting point should be to consider the needs of the child and the community rather than the nature of the material.

8.2 Client profile

A clear and detailed profile of each community is an essential prerequisite to effective stock provision (see 4.3.2). Staff should also get to know their communities by visiting schools and community institutions such as under-fives groups and youth clubs. They should talk to parents, teachers and, most importantly, the children themselves, and undertake user surveys to identify the client profile and needs, in the appropriate language and using skilled staff.

8.3 Collection development policy

Stock policy documents will vary from one authority to another, depending on the needs of the local community and the prevailing management climate. However, all should state clearly the objectives underlying stock provision, including the need to:

- communicate the pleasure and enjoyment that reading can bring
- enlarge and enrich the child's mind and imagination
- develop the child's use and understanding of language
- contribute towards the child's intellectual, emotional, psychological and social development
- prepare children to become lifelong readers and learners
- contribute positive images and help children reflect their own and others' cultural heritage
- provide for children's information needs, including support for both formal and continuing education
- offer opportunities to experience and experiment with new technologies.

8.4 Selection policy

A selection policy should be formulated which is agreed between library management and those responsible for selection. This should work within local authority policies, and address the needs of the local communities. The policy should address the following issues:

8.4.1 A recognition of demand

Though adult judgement will be the prime influence on stock for very young children, this must be balanced by a recognition of the child's demand. This implies:

- knowledge of demand on the part of all public service staff
- sufficient attention to known popular material
- recognition that some material requires promotion before demand can be fairly assessed

- feedback, to inform the selection stage
- willingness to talk to children and young people about what they want
- understanding of children's known tastes and preferences.

8.4.2 A judgement of need

Stock should be selected in the context of children's needs. Specialist knowledge is invaluable here in assessing the needs of:

- individual children
- categories of children (by age, ability and interest groups)
- all local children (the whole community, not users alone)
- all children (given the need for balance in issues such as race and gender).

8.4.3 A knowledge of materials

An intimate knowledge of, and enthusiasm for, children's literature and other materials must exist in order to:

- match materials closely to the needs of children
- recognize and promote original, good quality material
- answer the enquiries of parents and others.

A successful approach to selection should balance all these three elements. The undue dominance or neglect of any one of them will not achieve a stock which meets the service philosophy.

8.4.4 Selection criteria

These should include statements on:

- the issues of censorship and positive selection
- content, including such aspects as plot, style, characterization, currency, accuracy, bias (including racial and gender issues), vocabulary and age suitability
- physical format, including changing criteria in relation to format (e.g. CD-ROMs)
- the correct response to changing factors in the community, including educational issues (e.g. literacy initiatives, homework centres, National Curriculum requirements, use of IT)
- value for money.

Though selection policies for public libraries and schools library services may differ in detail and emphasis, there is a need for overall coordination between them. Many authorities operate reviewing and assessment schemes as a means of ensuring shared responsibility and alignment on the assessment and selection process. This also ensures participants remain knowledgeable and up to date about the publishing pattern of children's books, which is a cornerstone of specialist work. Modern technology is offering new approaches to this which can streamline selection processes.

8.4.5 Feedback

Positive efforts should be made to gather feedback from children about books. This could be achieved:

- in the course of book promotion
- through staff awareness and interest
- by incorporating children into the selection process
- through greater emphasis on the withdrawal process as a means of monitoring
- by monitoring requests.

8.5   Range

Children have a wide range of stock-related needs in terms of emotional, intellectual and aesthetic development, reading and comprehension levels, subject and interest areas. The needs of specific client groups (e.g. under-fives, young people, children of ethnic minority groups and those with special needs, as well as parents and other adults working with children) must be catered for. Needs will include material for educational and information purposes as well as for leisure and recreation. Stock should reflect the languages and cultures of the community or of countries such as Scotland and Wales.

8.6   Format

Formats may include board books, picture books, hardbacks, paperbacks, tactile books, comics and magazines, tactile material, sign language, large print, large format, books in Braille or ClearVision, community language material and dual text, sound recordings, spoken word, audiovisual material, video cassettes, computer software, CD-ROMs and toys. Factors to bear in mind will be the cost-effectiveness of various formats, the appeal factor, and the need to ensure that children are introduced to a wide range of literature.

8.7   IT provision

Libraries should consider providing CD-ROMs for loan, as well as keeping collections for use in the library. Collections may include games, living books, dictionaries, encyclopaedias, music, language learning and a range of non-fiction subjects.

Consideration should also be given to children's access to Open Learning collections, where much material is relevant to young people (e.g. job searching, basic skills, GCSE packages).

Children should be given access to automated library catalogues which are either simplified or have straightforward search facilities.

Whatever form of IT is being considered, it must be secure, as children can and will get into local authority systems if the 'fire walls' which protect the system are not solid enough.

An overall IT policy should be part of, or sit beside, the collection development policy. Authorities have a role in providing and promoting access to current technology and in enabling full use of this technology to access information in all appropriate formats. While IT is best seen as another item of stock to provide information, an IT policy is valuable. This should identify the objectives of providing IT, budgetary implications, staff training, information handling skills support, selection criteria, the different sources (e.g. CD-ROMs, public browser terminals, the Internet, local information databases) and the role of IT in such developments as homework centres.

8.8 Size of stock

At least one member of staff in every library should know the total stock and the shelf stock; these will vary according to the size of library and community served. The *Model statement of standards* for public library services (The Library Association, 1995)[1] recommends that two items per head of population should be used as a minimum. Stock should take account of:

- the abilities and interests of children throughout the age range
- local needs
- sufficient choice within each stock area.

Over-concentration on stock size can, however, lead to tired, unattractive libraries, because staff maintain their stock size rather than editing down to what is used.

8.9 Stock proportions

It is necessary to establish proportions of stock (e.g. picture books, early reading books, stories for independent readers, paperbacks, information books, reference, and young peoples material). Key points to consider are:

- the number of loans in each category
- the relationship of stock to client profile
- the balance between books and non-book materials (e.g. cassettes, computer software, magazines, toys etc.)
- the amount of material available to the user by category at any one time.
- the relationship of stock to the size and nature of service points.

8.10 Budget

Recommendation 8 of the LISC report *Investing in children*[2] reads:

> The percentage of the total materials budget applied to services for children and young people should be determined locally and should be at least the same as the percentage of children and young people in the population served. The percentage should be determined and should be subject to regular review.

This policy should then be expanded to include considerations of usage, wear and tear and average cost of items. The specification should recommend how the library should profile this budget against each category to ensure stock levels are maintained. This is where the local targets will vary from the standard.

8.11 Maintenance plan

Once stock proportions and budget allocations have been established, a maintenance plan is crucial. This should determine the number of new volumes or budget allocation required each year to maintain an appropriate level of provision in each category, either in one library or at all service points. Key factors will include:

- regular weeding of old and out of date stock, and monitoring for repair
- the shorter than average life expectancy of certain formats (e.g. picture books) leading to an especially high turnover
- new developments (e.g. stock for new libraries, new formats, introduction of IT etc.) which will require additional initial funding and a permanent increase in maintenance levels.
- special arrangements such as historic collections of children's books or last-copy policies, and the need for them to be clearly documented.

8.12 Stock circulation

To ensure that stocks remain relevant and attractive, a policy for stock exchange and circulation should be established, particularly for material that is quickly 'read through' (e.g. cassettes, videos, hardback fiction or particular subject areas). It is essential that a consistent and realistic withdrawals policy should operate.

8.13 Evaluation

The effectiveness of stock policies should be evaluated as part of an on-going process. The means of undertaking such evaluation can include:

- stock surveys
- user feedback
- questionnaires
- focus groups, unobtrusive testing, observation and talking to children
- monitoring of requests.

Use should also be made of statistical data.

References

1 Library Association, *Model statement of standards*, Library Association, 1995.
2 Library and Information Services Council (England), *Investing in children*, (DNH Library Information Series No. 22), HMSO, 1995.

9 Promotion

9.1 Introduction

Promotion is a vital part of service delivery and is not something to be 'added on'. Its purpose is:

- to recruit new library users
- to introduce books and reading
- to foster literacy
- to ensure library resources are fully used
- to offer opportunities for user education
- to enhance the image of the library
- to exploit all the different services of the library, including IT.

Promotion to children should be an integral part of the strategies for promoting the whole service. It should be built into service development at the planning stage, ensuring the staff have the appropriate skills and resources. Authority-wide promotions should be coordinated through the central specialist unit or section. A policy for local events is desirable which allows flexibility for a local response whilst maintaining agreed promotional standards.

9.2 Common factors

All library promotion should:

- meet clear objectives
- be targeted to defined audiences
- convey a clear message
- be cost-effective in the use of money, materials and staff time
- use the most effective and appropriate medium for the intended audience and the agreed objectives
- be professional in its appearance and delivery
- be assessed for impact and effectiveness
- be appropriate to the community served
- be adequately financed.

In addition, print-based publicity should use clear, appropriate and jargon-free language. It needs to be professional in appearance and designed to appeal to the client group. Where appropriate the use of the authority's graphics unit should be considered.

9.3 Target group

One of the particular factors affecting the promotion of children's library services is the variety of target audiences. Each of these offers different promotional opportunities, which need to be carefully thought through. The key target groups are as follows:

- *children* of all ages and intellectual and physical abilities and from a wide range of cultural backgrounds;
- *parents and other carers* – a vitally important group, particularly in reaching young children of pre-school age;
- *teachers*, who play a crucial role in the continued liaison between public libraries and schools;
- *governing bodies*, who influence an integrated strategy and can be important in school and public library use;
- *staff*, both within the libraries and across the local authority in general;
- *elected members*, who should be kept informed of developments and initiatives and be made aware of the importance of children's services;
- *the profession*, using promotional opportunities that
  - communicate ideas and initiatives to other colleagues
  - raise/sustain the profile of library work with children
  - raise the profile of the local authority.

9.4 Forms of promotion

9.4.1 The library building

The library building itself will convey a clear message about the service provided. Its external appearance, including any signing provided, should give a positive image of the service, and an attractive and welcoming interior environment should reinforce this. Matters such as guiding, display, furnishings and layout are an integral part of the promotional process. All these elements are of special significance with regard to children, to whom immediate visual impact is all-important.

9.4.2 Library vehicles

The promotional opportunities offered by library vehicles should be recognized. Mobiles and library buses make library services more accessible to a wider community, and may be used to target particular client groups such as pre-school children or isolated communities. In addition, a bright, colourful, exterior design on vehicles will considerably enhance their appeal to children.

9.4.3 Staff

In their daily contact with users, staff have a significant role to play in promotion, and this should be emphasized in training. For example, when enrolling new members, staff should introduce them to the range of services which are available to them. When dealing with enquiries, staff should take the opportunity to explain how the library is arranged and how to find information.

9.4.4 Contact with groups

Liaison with schools, pre-school groups, youth clubs and other organizations may take place in the library or involve staff making visits in the community. Both forms of promotion are particularly important because:

- they offer a direct way of appealing to children
- they afford special opportunities for talking to 'captive audiences'
- the detailed literature knowledge of specialist staff creates unrivalled opportunities to promote the stock (e.g. by book talks and storytelling)
- they are cost-effective and offer contact with a high proportion of potential library users
- they offer opportunities for immediate feedback and response.

Within the library, such promotion also offers the opportunity to:

- introduce the range of services and demonstrate how to use the library effectively
- introduce a range of information sources such as books, computers and multimedia material
- promote fiction and encourage reading.

Visits by staff to groups in the community may additionally offer:

- deposit of collections of books and other materials at various centres and establishments
- promotional activities such as storytelling to children who may not have the opportunity to visit the library
- opportunities to reach non-traditional users through activities and exhibitions in shopping centres, offices, factories, post-natal clinics etc. in order to contact parents and children who do not belong to groups.

9.4.5 Events and activities

Events and activities are a significant element in library work with children and should always have a clear purpose. Such events may take place during term time or during school holidays. Events may be directly book-related (e.g. author talks, storytelling, book weeks, holiday reading trails) or may include activities (e.g. puppet shows, drama and IT workshops) designed to create a positive image of the library. When deciding priorities for activities, the 'common factors' listed earlier in this chapter (see 9.2) should be studied objectively.

9.4.6 Displays and exhibitions

For children's services, displays and exhibitions offer exciting promotional opportunities. Here are two examples:

- book promotion to maximize the impact of attractive cover designs and to spotlight features of the stock such as fiction themes, recommended authors, topical subjects etc.
- displays of work from local schools and other agencies/organizations to attract parents and children.

9.4.7 Publicity

When producing publicity, careful thought must be given to issues such as format, appropriate language, illustrations, layout, house style, quantity, and distribution.

Visual impact and size of print are particularly important features. Items which particularly appeal to children, such as stickers, badges and bookmarks, may be useful forms of promotion. Non-print formats should also be considered such as video, audio tapes, Braille and technology such as the Internet.

The potential for press, radio and television coverage either locally or nationally should always be considered. This form of media coverage may be used to publicize forthcoming events or new services, or to create a high profile for children's library services. A strong selling point is the fact that children are frequently seen as 'media attractive' in the eyes of news editors looking for material. Effective promotion is still essential if this interest is to be turned into a specific presence and resultant coverage. If the authority has a marketing or public relations unit, their specialist advice and skills should be used.

Children's libraries: a reading list

This reading list is intended as an introduction to many of the areas of concern to children's libraries. With changes in local authority provision taking place on a regular basis, it is inevitable that some of the examples will no longer be applicable. However, most of the references share the crusading attitude which is typical of the best of those working in this field.

Essential reading

Department of National Heritage, *Investing in children: the future of library services for children and young people*, London, HMSO, 1995. ISBN 0 11 701994 1.
> Undoubtedly the most important report on children's library services for some time. Useful summaries are provided in *Library Association record*, **7** (4), April 1995, 214-7 and *The bookseller* 10 March, 1995, 40. The implications of the report are discussed by Judith Elkin and Debbie Denham in *The new review of children's literature and librarianship*, **1**, 1995, 13-33.

Library and Information Statistics Unit (various editors). A *survey of public library services to schools and children in England and Wales*. Loughborough, LISU, annual.
> An important way to view changes that have taken place from year to year is to compare figures or basic services. This annual survey has been produced since 1989, enabling the reader to see relatively easily patterns of change and development. A summary of the 1995-96 survey can be found in *School librarian*, **44** (4), November 1996, 143.

Elkin, Judith and Lonsdale, Ray (eds.), *Focus on the child: libraries, literacy and learning*, London, Library Association Publishing, 1996. ISBN 1 85604 109 3.
> This is probably the most comprehensive and concise account of the provision of children's services since Janet Hill's book (see below). Topics covered range from the theoretical, such as child development, to the practical, such as stock selection.

Hill, Janet. *Children are people: the librarian in the community*, London, Hamish Hamilton, 1973. ISBN 0 241 02243 6.
> Although many of the examples used in this seminal work are dated, the pioneering thesis that children are of such exceptional importance that their library services should be of the highest quality, makes it still a major work.

Williams, Alec, 'Towards the Millennium: children's and schools' librarianship in the year 2000', *New library world*, **96** (1124), 1995, 27-31.
> An extremely important article which looks in a clear sighted but still enthusiastic way at how children's library services may have changed by the end of the century.

Well worth reading

Shepherd, Jennifer, 'A crisis of confidence: the future of children's work', *International review of children's literature and librarianship*, **1** (1), 1986, 22–32.

Shepherd, Jennifer, 'Past imperfect, future indefinite', *International review of children's literature and librarianship*, **2** (2), 1987, 65–81.

Two well-argued and timely examinations of the purpose of children's librarianship. Although many of the circumstances quoted have changed, these articles are still worth reading for their perceptive conclusions on service provision.

Edmonds, Diana and Miller, Jane. *Public library services for children and young people: a statistical survey*, London, British Library, 1990. (Library and Information Research Report 72). ISBN 0 7123 3195 6.

The data for this was collected in the early and mid-1980s so it is probably not going to be of much relevance in today's climate. The second part of the book, however, is still of considerable interest, showing the wide variation in service provision between local authorities.

Special clients

Heaton, Jo (ed.), *Never too young. Volume I Library services to pre-school children and their carers*, Newcastle-under-Lyme, Youth Libraries Group, 1991. ISBN 0 946581 13 9.

A practical introduction to provision for the under-fives. Subjects include design, storytelling, bilingualism, special needs and provision for travellers, described mainly through case studies.

Hill, Linda and Pain, Helen, 'Young people and public libraries: use, attitude and reading habits; a survey of 13–16 year olds in Nottinghamshire', *International review of children's literature and librarianship*, **3** (1), 1988, 26–40.

Teenage users of libraries in Nottinghamshire were asked for their perceptions of the services provided and for suggestions for improvement. Comparisons are also made with similar surveys carried out in two other authorities.

Kinnell, Margaret, 'Far horizons: international perspectives on libraries and reading for teenagers', *International review of children's literature and librarianship*, **9** (2), 1994, 73–87.

The text of the 1994 Esme Green Memorial Lecture, this is an extremely useful summary of debates on library provision for teenagers, mainly in the UK. The international element of the subtitle is concerned mainly with the USA.

Lewins, Helen and Renwick, Frances, Barriers to access: libraries and the pre-school child in one English county', *International review of children's literature and librarianship*, **4** (2), 1989, 85–106.

An examination of the provision (including stock, activities and physical access) for the under-fives in one library authority. Wide variations were found between individual libraries, suggesting a lack of policy.

Marshall, Margaret R., *Handicapped children and books*, London, British Library, 1986. (British National Bibliography Research Fund Report 20). ISBN 0 7123 3067 4.

Marshall, Margaret, *Managing library provision for handicapped children*, London, Mansell, 1991. ISBN 0 7201 2078 0.

Margaret Marshall, an Eleanor Farjeon medal winner, has long been recognized as a passionate advocate for comprehensive provision for children with special needs. The first book is a survey of provision in the mid-1980s as well as a depiction of the National Library for the Handicapped Child, while the second book is more concerned with the management of special needs within libraries.

Matthews, David A. and Lonsdale, Ray, *Library and book services to children in hospital*, Aberystwyth, Department of Information and Library Studies, University of Wales, 1990. (British Library R & D report 6004). No ISBN.

A comprehensive survey of library provision in children's hospitals which suggests there should be more cooperation between service providers.

Neill, Lorna and Johnson, Ian M., 'Information for unemployed teenagers', *International review of children's literature and librarianship*, 6 (2), 1991, 95–117.

A survey of provision in three areas of Scotland. It was found that all three were providing information for unemployed teenagers but only one was successful in making this service known to many non-users of the library.

Wilkes, Bob, 'Library services for city children: a case study of Bradford, England', *International review of children's literature and librarianship*, 1 (2), 1986, 12– 26.

Although circumstances have changed since the publication of this article, it is still a useful examination of the various services provided (including under-fives provision and a special library for teenagers) which comes to a number of conclusions about service provision still relevant today.

Physical design

Dewe, Michael, *Planning and designing libraries for children and young people*, London, Library Association Publishing, 1995. ISBN 1 85604 100 X

A comprehensive guide to children's library planning which gives consideration to location, accommodation, furniture and equipment as well as to policy decisions, committees and teams.

Staff training

Kempster, Grace, 'Motivating staff in public library services to children and young people', *International review of children's literature and librarianship*, 3 (2), 1988, 9–125.

Based on work in three London boroughs, this survey examines attitudes of both children's specialists and non-specialists towards children's librarianship. Different levels of motivation were perceived.

Collection development

Blenkin, Sarah and Lewins, Helen, 'Collection management in British children's libraries: a report of five case studies', *Collection management*, **13** (4), 1990, 77-87.
It is always extremely useful to look at how differing authorities tackle the question of stock development, a fundamental aspect of children's librarianship. This article compares and contrasts the way five different authorities tackle the question.

Everall, Anne, 'Book selection for children: the critical question', *Youth library review*, **16**, 1993, 5-10.
This article examines the particular issues which have to be addressed in stock selection. These are particularly important in times of dwindling resources.

Eyre, Gayner and Rippingale, Ray, 'Managing stock for young people in Derbyshire', *Youth library review*, **17**, 1994, 8-12.
A description of the principles behind stock selection in a large county service.

Lonsdale, Ray and Everitt, Jean, 'Breaking down the barriers: the provision of modern foreign language material to young people in public libraries in the UK', *Journal of librarianship and information science*, **28** (2), 1996, 71-81.
A survey of the provision of children's material not produced in English. Levels of provision were either low or non-existent. Recommendations are given for future provision.

Lonsdale, Ray and Wheatley, Alan, *The provision of audiovisual and computer materials to young people by British public libraries*, London, British Library, 1990. (British National Bibliography Research Fund Report 49). No ISBN.
A comprehensive survey of non-book material provided in children's libraries. Summaries of the report are given in *International review of children's literature and librarianship*, **5** (3), 1990, 159-79 and **6** (1), 1991, 31-55.

Promotion

Eyre, Gayner (ed.), *Making quality happen: a practical guide to promoting your library*, Newcastle, Youth Libraries Group, 1994. ISBN 0 94658 17 7.
A deliberately practical set of case studies designed to encourage promotion and giving an abundance of suggested activities. Particularly useful for library workers who are new to children's work.

Thorpe, Dina, *Reading for fun: a study of how parents and librarians encouraged children aged 9-12 to read for enjoyment*, Bedford, Cranfield Press, 1988. ISBN 0 947767 91 6.

An extremely comprehensive description of family reading groups, a scheme whereby children, parents and professionals come together to read and discuss books.

Reading list supplied by Keith Barker, Deputy Librarian, Westhill College, Birmingham, and acknowledged with thanks.